EPIC POE

THE GOLDPRINT OF THE ARCHE

HEINRICH DITTRICH is a South-African writer, composer, and artist. Born in 1993, Vereeniging, his childhood was spent in Vanderbijlpark, Gauteng, until his family moved to Secunda, Mpumalanga, where he started the first grade and spent the rest of his childhood. After High school he proceeded to study languages (including, English, French, German, Latin, and Spanish) at the North-West University in Potchefstroom, North West. This opened an opportunity for him to work in France as an English Language Assistant Teacher. After traveling back and forth between the two countries, he started teaching languages at High School. He is now pursuing the arts while working as a part-time teacher.

By Heinrich Dittrich

PROSE FICTION

A Candle Under the Water (2021)

POETRY

Hortus:
The Goldprint of the Arche (2023)
The Secrets of the Sacred Arms (2023)

CRITICISM

Towards Identifying a New Literary Genre: Stature—the Status (2021)
Perfeksioneer Afrikaans as Addisionele Taal (2023)

THE HORTUS

La Chanson des Mille Rêves

PRESENTED FROM THE

Prime Anamnesis

PART ONE

The Goldprint of the Arche

HEINRICH DITTRICH

HEINRICH DITTRICH

The Goldprint of the Arche

La Chanson des Mille Rêves

Symbolical Script

[INDEPENDENTLY PUBLISHED]

THE GOLDPRINT OF THE ARCHE

First published in 2023

SECOND EDITION: NOVEMBER 2023

Draft2Digital

Imprint: Independently published

Self-published

INTRODUCTION.

The Goldprint of the Arche was first self-published in February 2023. Its November 2023 second edition contains some revised verses, which brings the poem's scope more in line with what I genuinely want the entirety of the epic to represent.

The readers of the epic who are interested can find the changes made to this volume of *The Goldprint of the Arche* in *The Secrets of the Sacred Arms* under "Textual and Revisional Notes". Furthermore, the manuscript remains unedited by any other parties apart from myself.

About the manuscript

I completed the original version of the epic poem between 2017 - 2023, although I had produced some notes concerning its scope before then, as the idea had come to me before that time.

However, the poem's core only surfaced while I was working as an English Language Assistant Teacher in Strasbourg, France, around 2019. I was still unaware of what the whole thereof would turn out to be, and it would only be at the beginning of 2023 that I had finally completed the first draft of the entire poem. Nevertheless, it remains incomplete.

The reasons for this preliminary script are both conventional and contextual. For, though half of the first draft rhymes, the other part lays in free verse, while both have no accurate metre. Likewise, the scope of the poem needs a few minor adjustments.

Towards its finality, I completed it in what was a challenging time of my life. For this reason, I hope that if anybody who has ever struggled in their life would come to give their time and attention to indulge herein, it might stand as a beacon of enlightenment. And if not. Then, at least have an enjoyable story to read in epic verse.

Inspirations and motivations

It was - and still is - a work in progress; this tale that grew in my imagination until it became what it is this day. There are as many things as there aren't to coerce a person into a strenuous task, such as writing a story. And, of all the things I can mention that have inspired and motivated me to achieve this dream, there is but one thing essential to note regarding this text—the incompleteness of ancient calligraphy. It is then that same fragmented history that holds many enigmas.

From religious texts and mythologies, legends and fairytales, conspiracies to sacred geometry, the unspoken truth remains. And from its comparison, I could draw a parallel between those times and our lives and mine. There are many things we need help understanding. Many answers we need to find. And though I wouldn't call myself an expert in these affairs, it is my curiosity that greatly inspired me and motivated me to discover some truth through fiction.

The scope of the poem

Standing in my father's garden, stargazing, I had vivid fantasies replaying time over and again in my mind until the pieces of the puzzle finally came together in a cohesive whole that made sense—the epic tale of the decay of Mars into the red planet and the formation of Earth, and all the ancient history that preceded these events.

The Goldprint of the Arche thus discloses the mythological background of this ancient history: the phenomenon surrounding the most significant, yet discreet, war known by man—the first war between good and evil in the heavens. This origin thus give rise to all proceeding experiences.

Arrangements and Prosody

From its minor components to its entirety, I've built the *Hortus* like a puzzle out of the Fibonacci sequence of numbers.

The manuscript thus halves itself into two primary sections, where each section further splits into three parts. Finally, each part divides itself into five scrolls or books, each consisting of eight poems.

Thus, *The Goldprint of the Arche* is the first part of the foremost five ancient scrolls presented by the Prime Anamnesis in the Hortus.

Moreover, I wrote the epic poem primarily in heroic couplets.

*

But without further ado… There awaits you other surprises in the poem.

HEINRICH DITTRICH, 2023
INTRODUCTION TO THIS EDITION OF
THE GOLDPRINT OF THE ARCHE

CONTENTS.

III. THE SECOND SCROLL OF CREATIONS

IV. VESICA PISCES

V. SEVERANCES

By what's gone, shall we ask to find beauty again?

PREFACE.

EVERYTHING has a divine beginning…

Mythological, miraculous, epical, *The Goldprint of the Arche* is the curtain-raiser to the epic saga about the decay of Mars into the red planet. There are many myths, legends and ancient history surrounding this phenomenon. And though the ending is disclosed, it does not reveal all there is to be known. For so are secrets concealed. The histories are made discreet. And the truth ultimately goes forgotten in time.

The Goldprint of the Arche gives the mythology encompassing Mars's fall.

The Goldprint of the Arche

SCROLL I

The Author's Invocation of the

MUSES

THUS

The Scroll of Muses Marked

INSPIRATIONS

[ARGUMENT]
The scroll of inspirations is focused primarily on invoking the muses and setting the themes for the scrolls and books to come. For both the reason of the epic poem's scope as well as the purpose thereof, the first invocation precedes the muses' reply to these ideas. After a second invocation, the muses introduce the epic tale.

1. The Grand Manifesto for Great Remedies

WHY wherefore tragedies of such cruel world
Has left me later as I have been hurled.
'Twas once a beauty, thought I'd truly known
That has left its significance alone.
I see no more good in this lonely road,
Because the sins and vices that it showed.

Thus, in rev'rence, I see my father's garth,
Too sensitive to touch this burning hearth:
I feel no more such mercy 'pon my soul,
Of this that left my heart a vacant hole.
So wasted, sweating in these desert lands,
I'm faithless with my blood on my two hands;
I'm hopeless, as I've fallen on my knees,
Of all this beauty 't seems that I can't seize;
So lovelorn tears drop from my blinded eyes,
As I concede to this despair of cries.
Howe'er unpolished, I'll still raise my laud:
That battered I am but a man, not God!
(And God deserves all glory and of prayer,
To whom this floral symbol can't compare.)
And thus remain my destiny of aim:
For this towards all better things proclaim.
This metaphor, then only but a play:
The quest for truth—aesthetics of good way.

2. The First Invocation: An Orison: My Lament to the Muses

BEGET in me again such splendour art,
O muses, hear my calling cries impart.
Of yearning ardour, I cannot compare,
For it remains an arduous affair.
I have but one pant left inside of me,
O muses, that I may beseech of thee:
That through me sagas be awarned anew,
For I desire a glance of your fair view.
I have but only heard about all 'f you,

And rules of yours to vanquish feels of blue.
They say you are as pure as driven snow,
With valued traits all virtues worth to know;
And with physiques to charm one from the vile,
O, into beauty's comfort all worthwhile.
O, muses always live and love and laugh,
For you are good and beauty on behalf.
O, sing! O, sing to me! I beg your grace,
From all those places you with joy embrace.
The sound of your sweet silence scorches much,
It was a beacon bright at once in touch.
Yet now that brightness you have put aside
Became a fiery torch, which is no guide;
It burns much deeper than the other sores,
Betrayed, I am, to fight alone my wars.

3. The First Response: The Interpretations of Music

HIS voice crescendoed as the breaths of wind,
Discerned by hearts and little by the mind.
His voice arose on th' edge before my mess,
And thundered life in me, releasing stress.
As keen the howl of wolfs in even air,
He sounded natures instruments with care:

"O, heed! Of what my secret notes conceal:
They speak of the return of the great zeal.
Unlock my mysteries of melodies,
You shall thus know divinest harmonies."

4. The Second Response: The Sight of Clairvoyance

BEHIND the shapes of nature's lovely veil,
Of opened clouds like curtains for hail.
Her revelation thus revealed the stars,
Within the constellations: my 'nner Mars.
The sight of goodness in the middle-night,
The visions striking bolts as clear as light:

"Behold! My art can show you all the way,
One gaze—my hope in every darkened day.
Be gone! Whate'er your artistry may cloud,
So naught can halt your fair creation vowed."

5. The Third Response: The Intimacy of a Touch

SHE came to hoist me to my seamless stance,
And took my hand to lure me from this trance.
It was the faith of wind I've heard before,
A touch so sharp like sunlight on the shore.
It showed me even trees would take her hands
To dance with her through storms she too commands.
This vantage point about all life makes sense,
About life's growth that breaking norms commence:

"O, take my hand and feel your gracious poise,
And let me lead you in the journey's joys,

Around perfection in the grand design,
That I may have this dance within this shrine."

6. The Fourth Response: The Word of the Divine

HER declaration came without abhor
And deep it spoke into my conscious core.
'Twas spoken louder than the common tongue,
Yet still unheard but understood among;
Of greatest things within translations lost,
Restored in me the affirmations glossed:

"Of much great lies you have been told by some,
Who turns my words for more they can become.
To change the course of the mean moods of men,
Let me make hearts thus rather speak again."

7. The Second Invocation

BEGET in me and do not ever cease,
O muses, to disclose me to the peace.
And only if I had more time to give,
That this then too could have come to outlive.
This orison that beauty be reborn,
Within me that through me it is adorn.

Enlighten me the trav'llers of the skies,
Whose winsome wings allowed their flight to rise;

And those allowed to fare in waters deep,
To swim the seas with fins divine they keep;
And those who walked the plains of mighty trees,
Whose hearts were pure and kind in nature's ease.
Yet in allotted time they're all deceived
By dreadful terrors of the dark—they grieved.
Thus, kings and queens and gods of them were made,
With blood and sweat and tears that had them prayed.
But those reborn in light had shared their hope,
Who made amends to keep the epic scope.
With secret bloodlines in the mix for years,
as all awaited desperately for hears.

8. A Choir of Muses Sings

WE ought beget in you such art anew,
Where graceful things may grow to be e'er true.
Your wish for time shall incomplete remain,
So try as best you can in time's domain.
In medias res is your chaos now,
In a coherent whole we will endow.
Of all the knowledge kept the silent tone,
Thus let this universal truth be known:
The great divine remains from us concealed,
And yet, by this will it itself reveal:
The sacrifice of our own blood and tears
And sweat, bears forth the secrets of the years.
As we were those who were awakened first,
We were there too to witness every burst.
Thus, we'll remove such vices—worst of man,

As we recall, this is how it began:

SCROLL II

The Myth of Hortus'

I CREATIONS

THUS

The Scroll Marked Creations, the First

[ARGUMENT]

An interpretation of creation: The first Scroll of Creations introduces the beginning of the process of reviving Mars. In doing so, it sends the reader back in time by telling the origins of creation. This scroll is inspired by sacred geometry, as a type of blueprint of formation, to follow the succession of creation from the one point (i.e., consciousness and energy) to the bearing of the fruit of life carried by the tree of life.

9. Reminiscence of the Terrestrial Constellations

WE sing the song about a thousand dreams
To you, and thus to you evoke its themes.
Behold! Express your view upon the sky,
And fix your gaze on cosmic realms of high.
There hides alluring tales of old as well,
Of matters and of ages that excel.

Yet raise not your concern of its depart,
For better beauty bound its truthful heart.
And sometimes we can seem upon the end,
As if the end be first and there be spend.
Although the cruise of life it all excels,
Of secrets to the end, the end not tells.
Thus, this not only tells of the red field,
For in that course much secrets are concealed.
Behold! Express your view upon the sky,
And fix your gaze on cosmic realms of high.
A globe, adays, as rusty red as gore,
With a dry face that wraps a dust decor.
And circled erst by graceful moons, now 'bused,
Once, ever green, and clear blue that amused.
O, now it lies in shadows of the stars,
The world too known by the mere name of Mars.

10. The Origin:
The Prime Mover

BEFORE the part of such a beauty pure,
Of clusters and of deities secure,
The void could not come closely to compare
This very much significant affair.
Behold! There was the aeon of, thus, Om
And all the ages came from this aplomb.
Hence, ere the set-up of eternity,
There was but consciousness' divinity.
As the unique of wind, it was alike,
So could its radiant energy strike.
And though there was no face to scrutinize,

Yet fit to seem its depth with blinded eyes;
And ne'ertheless, no flesh to grasp a hold,
This conscious precious more than that of gold;
And still, no smell of it was in the air,
One would pursue its nudeness anywhere;
No lips to kiss nor tongue to taste,
No sea nor field could fill what it embraced;
And in vast silence there around it moved,
It did not need a word to be improved.
No boundless space it need'd to be contained,
No nothingness it need'd to be explained,
No void it need'd to breathe and keep this free,
For in itself and out it merely be.
With this strange sense you knew that it was there,
They are, called Hortus—this their credit air.

11. The Awakening of the Vesica Pisces

FROM consciousness, there's no conditions set,
For that their love was pure, which was first met,
That for the first of realms they knew to be,
An unseen realm of hope of pure degree:
The eyes of hope that showed the crate of deeds,
This was the first of times that Hortus heeds.
And there in that first realm where much is bound,
The Goldprint of the Arche they too found:
The parallel of esse 'twas the same,
As if it's the pure heart of hope in frame.
As compass for all time and space, it stood,
Like a design of every little good;
The layout of a single grain of sand

To the fair concept of itself was planned;
And all of this for all there could begin,
A mirror of the possible within.
So therefore, in their likeness as the wind,
With good and great and perfect faith combined,
The first awakening came into be'ng,
And mindful of what they all were agree'ng:
Tillandsia, Nymphaea, Sedges, Rose,
These were their mighty names that them disclose.
They were awakened first with great intent,
For the good muses they all represent.

12. The Creation of Nothingness

THUS Hortus, in their parts, considered fame,
For the creation to begin its claim,
Yet for the things they knew they swithered dear,
The Goldprint of the Arche was e'er clear:
It had perceived the good and love of things,
Yet with much evil and of fear it brings.
It did not show which shall of which destroy,
For that remained for each one to employ.
And for this reason, Hortus made their choice:
For love will conquer all and thus rejoice.
And so it was as it commenced the realm
Of nothingness that Hortus came to helm.

13. The Seed and Egg of Life

FOR in the nothingness that Hortus sought,
The first of elements divine they brought.
Thus, in the vastness of the infinite,
The space of void to change was imminent.
The first of times and ages then record,
As Hortus breathed as sharp as an edged sword.
(And thus the first of aeons came complete,
That pathed the way for imminent replete.
And so the age the first creations came
Within the aeon of creations' aim.)
A cut intense that went through all the void,
And from it soared a sound that had employed
A mystic fire of vibrant heat and light
That flowed in tensive waves and shocking smite.
And so, a chaos born by this effect.
However, consciousness' hands swiftly set,
As streams of liquid, smoke-like light, they flow,
Out of their realm, complete to catch the foe.
And as a seed of life to pollinate,
Its air's intent was thus set to create.
This tamed and calmed the chaos from the strife,
Into a beautiful, bright egg of life.

14. The Tree of Life

THUS all the elements appeared as one,
As th' egg soon split, new atom shapes begun.
So aethereal space was there around,

When fire vaporised, the waters bound,
And so the air and skies had made its den,
And from the skies the waters rained again
That then below erodes the fire's heat,
And formed the elements of earth concrete.
Thus now a limited and flat façade,
Of this suspended in the space as quad.
Therefore, the first of souls were perfect made,
The second then awaited the next grade.
Then Hortus spoke again with all their might,
A sound of wind from silence and delight.
And soon a glowing bud sprout up from earth,
As th' elements then nurtured its good worth.
It grew into a tree which stemmed in two,
Where there on opposite of sides, they grew.
Their shimm'ring branches then had sprouted out
To give the brightest light in space throughout;
With trunk to branch as golden topaz shone,
With leaves as emeralds e'er green they'd grown.
And though together they were named of life,
Alone: of spirit and of ethos rife.

15. The Flower of Life

AN endless season of the spring commenced:
The trees with blooming flowers they dispensed.
And all the knowledge and of life they keep,
Within their vibrant colours soon to reap.

16. The Fruit of Life

SO same the trees, they were, that by the next
Were they opposed from their appearance vexed:
One bore a fruit, a single golden globe,
The kin, five clustered diamonds in a strobe.
So there they bloomed and grew all that is good
Of many merits where they firmly stood.

SCROLL III

The Myth of the Vesica Pisces'

II CREATIONS

THUS

The Scroll Marked Creations, the Second

[ARGUMENT]

The second scroll of creations follows the creation of the third realm by Hortus, and the proceeding creation within the second realm by the Vesica Pisces. Furthermore, not only does it conclude the formation of the three realms, but it also tells the climatic story of the first rebellion that resulted in the creation of the beings.

17. Hortus' Creation: The Creation of Botanica

THUS now there were three realms: where one was fixed,
The other two were thus together mixed.
The first was where the realm of hope is bound,
The Goldprint of the Arche was there found.
The second was the realm of th' elements,
The tree of life there gave enlightenments.

The time came for a third to take its shape,
So Hortus made another world t' escape.
Dividing physical from the divine,
The third came into an extant design.
The second from the third was thus concealed,
Though from the third all was revealed.
(And Hortus was th' origin of e'ergy,
Who sourced all realms of this divinity.)
Of its description much remains untold,
For non could enter with a coin or gold.
Yet there are sounds that speak of its allure:
A world of gold and gems and good and pure.
With seas of beryl blue and suns of gold,
With silver moons and fields of emerald,
And there is built a castle on the high,
On top of ruby mountains in the sky.
And vacant and unfriendly it was not,
For in its midst there sojourned yet a lot,
For all the souls were there complete and found,
From rock to plant to animals around.
And then there were the fourth of souls as well,
Who'd their own hierarchy sets excel;
There were some souls as guardians at hand,
With great and winsome wings for their demand.
And then there were those souls as children loved,
To benefit from this realm, they were behoved.
Thus in the palace there were fifteen thrones,
The three put in the centre Hortus owns,
And four put for the muses on the right,
Whilst eight put on the left for their own might:
The first was for the keeper of faith good,
The second for the virtues and their mood,
The third protected the first realm of hope,

The fourth o'er war and joy's appointed scope,
The fifth was for forgiveness and of grace,
The sixth was granted knowledge to embrace,
The seventh held eternal life in hand,
The eight protected the third realm's expand.
And each had legions which below them placed,
The Goldprint of the Arche had so traced.
Thus this was what Botanica became,
Of all the greatest beauty in one frame.

18. The Creation of the Four Worlds: The Cosmos, the Mars, the Seas, and the Skies

THOUGH evil was already there about,
The plan still needed to be pushed throughout:
Botanica's creation was complete,
The Vesica Pisces thus sent to meet,
The second realm where they thus now reside,
For a fair fate they'll very soon provide.
Thus this had come to mark the ending of
The first creation's age so set above,
A herald thus for what became the next,
The second age of the creation flexed.
And then he took the Goldprint from its realm,
For other hands thus it could overwhelm,
So Hortus only but this time had shared,
The Goldprint of the Arche thus declared.
They whole thereof to them he did not show,
But rather each received a part to know.
Thus each had seen a quarter of the scope.

For he had showed to them the eye of hope,
For them to carry on and to design
What Hortus once began in form divine.
Yet Hortus wanted Sedges to return,
Back to Botanica for his concern,
Whereas the trinity would have their due
To rule there in all that creation grew.
Thus, Sedges was then taken to the plains,
Where he could take the space for all his claims.
He saw and there revered all o'er the vast,
Far and below the trees all things to cast.
And so all that he came to learn of light,
He thus bestowed his powers and his might.
He took the vast and forged the whole of space,
He did, with glorious and wondrous grace.
Thus from the smallest drifting sphere above,
To every single system fixed in shove;
Each galaxy and cluster in its course,
So soon the universe had shown its force.
And as his world had come to be complete,
The Goldprint from him thus made its retreat.
Thus 'fore he went to Hortus to return,
He waited first to see his sisters' turn.
The second world was yet to be complete,
And by the fairest hands of Rose to meet.
But for she felt a sense of turn in greed,
She could not take her sis' space to proceed.
So soon the sibling met and had accords,
A covenant had sealed two worlds in wards:
By the first sign of the reshaping flat
Into a turning sphere by a plain plat.
Thus by the dance of their four loving hands,
There rose the surface from the waters sands,

That soon made deserts, shores and mountains rose,
Where florae came and forests all expose.
Then came the creatures all to walk the mars,
A paradise of green beneath the stars.
And so it was, she'd given back the piece,
The Goldprint of the Arche, once received.
While Rose made all nature's shapes aglow,
So too Nymphea's fancy set to show.
Thus lakes and seas were vast and waited fame,
And would be worthy of the great acclaim.
So she had made all water's beasts alive,
T' all plants with striking features she contrive.
And so it was, she'd given back the piece,
The Goldprint of the Arche, once received.
The last and fourth of worlds now being made,
Of what will endlessly be well displayed.
The harvest of the waters by the glow,
Had set in motion, nests of clouds to know.
Tillandsia then add'd to her design,
The gliding beasts in clouds to live and dine.
And there the clouds remained unmoved and fixed,
For all fowl kind that was there first transfixed.
And so it was, she'd given back the piece,
The Goldprint of the Arche, once received.
And so the worlds of Mars were all complete,
Thus Sedges saw the worlds and to accrete,
He graced his sisters with two gifts of peace:
Two moons for his creation to increase.

19. The Velvet Gate

THERE in Botanica, its guard was called
Into collect of something that enthralled.
He had to Hortus went without delay,
Where Hortus in a garden 'lone display.
And there was giv'n a task to him of key:
The Goldprint of the Arche to foresee.
And to conceal its po'er from every sight,
Into the archive's vault must come its might.
And yet upon a glance of this divine,
The guard had from his mantle torn a line,
To shield his eyes, and covered them with care,
And then he took the Goldprint on its fare;
And even then had his eyes grown red and dark,
For the small part he saw that made a mark.
Where there in the deep depths he had it placed,
Behind a Velvet Gate lest it's faced.

20. Sedges' Betrayal over Creation: The First Vice

THUS, Sedges idolized creation's flair,
Amused by all its beauty and things rare,
As his desire consumed him to become,
The one and only ruler t' all succumb.
His jealousy had clouded his decrees,
As he too wanted all his sisters' keys.
For all creation laid in mystery,
The Goldprint was the key to victory.

He went to find his sisters for control,
Demanding their small part of the great whole.

But they replied to him and said with care:
"Alas! Who's he? What question do you bare?
We have not what you seek so anymore,
We were to render it aback before.
The secrets thus now with creation lies,
Its powers are too precious for th' unwise."

His feelings furious, his views were vile,
So he let loose his wrath with much hostile.
And left them harmed and hurt without remorse,
Thus, to the darkness he had turned his course.
And in the secret darkness he prepared
Unspoken wickedness that somewhere flared.

21. The Dark Army Rises: Rebellion of the Infernal Brigade

SO now his eyes were fixed on better things,
For glory onto him more power brings:
One was the legion of the second realm,
Two was the tree of life all overwhelm.
Yet those beneath the sixth throne's fierce command,
They had no need to hear of his demand,
For they revered all of his powers fame,
They fell exalted into his acclaim.
And so their noxious nature was alike,
Of things that they in common thus dislike.
Revolt and blasphemy were their motif,

Of their supremacy they held belief.
Thus there on Mars they gathered in great force,
And on the highest mountain made th' endorse.
But of this mutiny stood out but one,
Their first commander had remained undone.
He tried to stop, convince, and fight this horde,
But of this crime of treason, they roared.
For he was overpowered and left stiff,
And they then through him from a soaring cliff.
Where on the bottom nature had him tamed,
Because of better things he was proclaimed.
It was the trinity of sisters' aid,
With cleansing water, breath of air, and shade.
They raised again of his strong hold and stance,
This mercy gave to him a second chance.
Thus, from the beating-break, he yet broke free
Towards Botanica as refugee.

There he sought Hortus' presence to explain,
Of all the incidents that were profane:
"There's mutiny in the next realm,
Alas! As I was taken from my helm.
O, how the legions have betrayed your grace,
And they will soon make here their wicked race."

Thus, not a moment spared of Hortus' law,
And ordered every legion's draw,
Yet of a single one had there remained
To guard Botanica and be sustained.
And yet before they're set there on their course,
So firstly Hortus had them reinforce,
That lest they bear of much ill fates and harms,
He had created them the sacred arms.

22. The Cursed Crusade

THE second part of Sedges' raid began,
The journey to the Goldprint was th' end plan,
And for he knew the function of much things,
He knew where he must his attention brings.
Thus the infernal brigade forged ahead,
There where the tree of life its branches spread,
And there they came to make it burn to dust,
So to declare their reign of their disgust.
Before they stood to watch the tree in flames,
Five fruit had Sedges plugged there from the frames.
Like diamonds they had shone before the pick,
That changed as other colours them now stick.
One was as golden as the sun's fair sight,
And two was ruby red, and three pearl white,
And four was clear as blue of the marine,
And five, an emerald, so was its green.
As pearls yet each their own of shapes to be,
As elements where they came from the tree.
And though unlike the Goldprint gives consent,
The Elements, the opposite content:
The secrets of creation they display,
Of that what truly is and surely stay.
And though alone they each was e'er profound,
If mixed their powers have but a great bound.
And thus the time had come of their long wait,
Of all to come, of all for their good fate.
Thus Sedges posed them down there on the front,
A hexagon they formed there for the stunt;
The tree as angle of the sixth apex,
And so was all prepared for a convex.

Thus half of the grand tree was first to burn,
As all threw fire for what they greatly yearn.
It was not long before it had revealed
The Goldprint sought and where it was concealed.
For in Botanica was their delight,
With whom it lied shall have a fight.
By mercy 'fore more ruin there were made,
The legions from Botanica came t' aid.
One half of the good tree was an ash grave,
Yet half of the good tree they came to safe.

"Behold! We have by Hortus' word arrived,
Of harm that's made shall thus now be revived.
O Sedges, once we called you brother dear,
But now it seems that you became of fear.
And all of you, who stand by his disgrace,
What does your true allegiance thus embrace?
Give up your fight and come with us away.
You are outnumbered one to six. Obey!"

Back to Botanica, they all thus went,
Surrounded by the legions, to repent.
Yet with surprise no comeback they had faced,
For the dark army's need to be replaced.

23. The First Great War: The War in Botanica

WHAT gives death glory in undying realms?
But pain, and tears, and torture at the helm.
Botanica, they entered cuffed in chains,

Secured by every guard, avoiding strains.
In front and left and right all stood prepared,
In bearing arms for these ill fates be spared.
Thus halted in a quod by glory's door,
They have arrived to give their plea of war,
Where they awaited Hortus to give sight,
And for that moment feeling time's worst might.
What gives death glory in undying realms?
But pain, and tears, and torture at the helm.
And what gives war the length of time to thrive?
If it be years, years passed in a brief strive.
As those of the infernal they became,
Thus so they came to show of their new name.
And Sedges stood there first to start with shakes,
Into a dragon fierce he then awakes.
He broke the chains and breathed fire in th' air!
Amazed, some guards regarded the affair
As a good sign to show their true belief,
And where their nature showed their true motif.
Thus now a third of all the legions turned,
The guards looked on and saw their brothers spurned.
A mystic flap of dragon wings made winds
That turned his army into blazing fiends.
What gives death glory in undying realms?
But pain and tears and torture at the helm.
A final battle seemingly commenced,
Of a great war whose end must yet be sensed.
One third against two thirds they fought,
A stint of time, yet th' end was dearly sought.
What gives death glory in undying realms?
But pain and tears and torture at the helm.
A war that's ripples had a deep effect,
Still felt through every realm as they project.

And so the dragon breathed its fire fierce,
Its aim: the castle doors through which it pierce.
Far was salvation, and yet not in sight,
The keeper of good faith, he had no fright.
He took his sword and brandished it with skill,
The dragon fiercely going for a kill.
The keeper's skills, superior and best
Had plunged the sword into the beast's big chest.
The dragon's form thus then from him departs,
And so away towards the ground he darts.
So Sedges fled into the open doors,
His rivals thus could him not stop from course,
For fiends attacked and blocked their good attempt,
Thus t' archives Sedges went to show contempt.
Where he thus found the guard of the third realm,
Behind the Velvet Gate for him to whelm.
And from behind the Velvet Gate he came,
And blindfolded, he did, with eyes aflame.
Without remorse his upper hand had struck,
The guard had no fair chance nor luck,

And on the floor he fell, yet not dismayed,
And thus from there he spoke e'en unafraid:
"Yet through this veil I've seen apart of light,
To you it only brings the darkened night.
How don't you understand the wiseman's word?
This knowledge shall thus let your death be herd.
What if you had the knowledge of the realms?
And yet you cannot comprehend this helm.
And e'en to influence of it you seek?
But in it, yet it shows to mark that peak.
And its destruction e'en you wish to cause?
A phoenix it becomes that ne'er withdraws.

For in it, yet it shows all things and sums,
A glance of it, the blinder you'll become."

"O, do not lecture me, you serving fool,
Of this that will become my greatest tool.
I've seen the realms into creations grow,
I have created one myself below.
Of this you are too weak and frail to wield,
For I've too seen a part of its great field.
Have you not thought what of you can become
If you can come to yield its power drum?"

And then he took the arm the guard had borne,
With force, so that the Velvet Gate be torn.
Yet though before he could reduce the gate,
He heard a once familiar voice of late.
So Hortus grandly entered the rare room,
And with him went away all of the gloom.

"O Sedges, by what have you grown to be?
Of you I've hoped for a sublime degree.
And tell me what have you created there?
My legions told me of your ill affair.
You seek of things that does not you conform,
And yet you think of things you can reform.
You had to fight these feels you feel inside,
But you, you'd rather have them you provide.
So you've betrayed me with your wicked plots,
And disobeyed me with you treason lots;
To me not only have you done this deed,
But onto you yourself, the good you reap.
I knew you e'en before you were awake,
You shouted out for me not you forsake.

So even then your conscious zeal out cried,
And I, I heard your cries and then replied.
So I agreed and let all to begin,
The sole consideration that you'll win:
The inner battle, and your peace be met,
That good in you shall thus the bad offset.
Because I know that good shall e'er prevail,
The beauty of the truth that much entail."

And thus he gave his smirkish of reply,
As he his wickedness all so deny:
"You speak of things from a high standing tide,
So though as if we all must you abide.
You ask me things as if I'm my desire,
You tell me things as if it me inspire.
Was that not our command (revolted he),
Creating each a part of space, I plea?"

And as he spoke his words then came alive,
As he then took the arm and made his strive.
The Velvet Gate thus sundered to reveal,
The whole of wonders it come to conceal.
He glanced upon it, blinder he became,
And yet allowed the dragon to reclaim.
But 'fore his transformation was complete
Had Hortus grounded it from its repeat:
With only a mere touch in swiftness act,
That left of him transfixed lest he react.
Then Hortus went to stand by his faint side,
And touched his shiv'ring body to abide.
And there he sent him into his exile,
The realm of hope, his prison for his vile.
Yet 'fore he had come to be sent away,

He lay and glanced upon the light's display:
The Goldprint thus to him reveal his fate,
As well as how he can of it negate.
And so he grabbed the first of things he could,
His presence ever fixed and thus withstood.
The Elements of Pearls still by his side
Fell to the ground; he disappeared and died.
Salvation was perceived through palace doors
That ended every battle of great wars.
For out stepped Hortus in his splendid state
To stop the fight without a grand debate.
And then he touched the surface of the land
As all changed back to normal as once planned.
Thus now the realms still laid in there fit set,
As Hortus had to dispute this great threat:
To settle this great clutter with fair grace,
And so he heard th' infernal brigade's case.
But still the fiends faithless act,
He ordered their imprisonment intact.
Thus those of mutiny were all detained,
In places shut and thus obscured retained.
And all the fiends who Sedges loyal served,
The tallest hill of Mars was them reserved.

24. Creations of the Beings

FOR what occurred inside this place of peace,
So Hortus called the sisters for increase.
For though he knew where Sedges thus reside,
He still lives on in mem'ries that him tied.
And thus, these memories could him bring back,

He needed all so to forget the plaque.
And though he might come to return someday,
His weakened state shall be his e'er decay.
Of this instruction rendered no excuse
Because of all that had been in misuse:
The great design of beings in effect,
A pledge of beauty—vices to correct.
And only Hortus could bring them alive,
His breath and soul and wind will all revive.
Thus first the race of embryophyte born.
Of men and women Rose came to adorn.
Who first lived under all the glowing stars,
And populated all the lands of Mars.
And there through all the ages they progressed,
With towns in th' east and north and south and west.
And after this was done to great extend,
There was awaiting something in the blend.
Thus from Nymphaea rose of her display:
The race of Algae in the seas gave way,
As mermen and mermaids, they too were known,
There in the seas that they have made their own.
The name of Lotus was the first thus called,
And as the ruler he was there installed.
In likeness of her image, he'd a fin,
Of beauty great and a pure heart, he'd win.
He swam amongst the fish with a lone eye,
In sadness and in ache with a faint sigh.
And for Nymphaea knew what this had meant,
For she foresaw such possible event,
She made some maidens, one he could elect,
But Lotus felt not, by this, an affect.
So from the surface rose a fort of gold.
For Lotus to behove and all behold,

For soon he shall thus find a true betroth,
First, he must mind the seas, she took an oath.
And after a grand gesture with fair Rose,
Because of the event that so disclose,
The maidens were thus called into collect,
For all the following to take effect:
In seas or on the land they may belong,
Where either choice will find them mates along.
And for their kiss and tears bore deep result,
Where'er they go, they shall bring great consult.
Tillandsia was last, for she too made,
Of those who had some winsome wings displayed:
The race of Ionantha flew the sky,
The airlads and airdames had come to fly.
There were those Ionantha of the high,
Who had specific purpose to apply.
And these their mighty names that them disclose:
Usneoides had there come to pose,
And Andreana and Bulbosa too,
So Butzii and Cyanea grew,
With Brachycaulos who were thus the last,
And they had those who's still to come surpassed.
Thus then she made the rest of all who glide,
And on the cloudy surface was their side.
And in a fort of glass, they came to live,
Where on and o'er the clouds was built this hive.
Thus, of these three original descents,
Were made immortal and without laments.
And as all ages need to meet their end
So were the second age and aeon spent.
And as they had thus come to their complete
It pathed the way for imminent replete.

SCROLL IV

The Lives and a Legend of the

VESICA PISCES

THUS

The Scroll Marked Vesica Pisces

[ARGUMENT]

The events described in this scroll transpired after the calling of the void and the creation of the third realm, and before the creation of the cosmos and the three worlds of planet Mars. The scroll of the Vesica Pisces describes Hortus nurturing the Vesica Pisces to become creators of their own in the second realm.

25. The View of Goodness

THE age of Hortus' shaping came to end,
And from his conscious realm he thus transcends.
In form that's true yet so mysterious,
Just like the wind; he was imperious.
To look upon the tree of life at hand,
A sight of beauty and of goodness stand.
And for he saw that all was safe and sound,
A perfect home for who will there be bound.

Thus he transcended to and fro again,
To bring their children down to decent den.
But though before the tree of life they saw,
They had explained to them of the new law.
There in Botanica they called the four,
The Vesica Pisces thus to explore.

"Tillandsia, Nymphaea, Sedges, Rose,
(So Hortus have commence to them expose)
Botanica has come to its complete,
Another realm there lies for us to meet.
Yet there you shall forget and start anew,
Be not afraid, I'll be there to accrue."

26. The Transcendence of the Vesica Pisces

THUS to the tree of life they all transcend,
For a new life where they will come to spend.
Their air was now maternal warm and kind.
With love that's unconditional defined.
And she was dressed in a white robe of silk,
Her hair and skin that glittered showed her ilk.
She held the infants in her arms devout,
Down to the tree that grew one fruit throughout.
The tree then turned and twisted with a clunk,
And there a door unfolded from its trunk.
They entered then the glowing tree to rest,
And where inside the tree which had them blessed,
For it grew them a bassinet of peace,
There in its court the children laid t' increase.
And from the tree she plugged them leaves to b' eased,

So they are swaddled and were made o'er pleased.
Their swelling hunger and great thrust were clenched,
For by the fruit of life they were thus drenched.
And whereby every night to them were sung,
A lullaby from an inspirit'd tongue.

27. The Tetrad Siblings

SHE raised them in and under the liv'ng tree,
As elegant from where they came to be.
From infants to four children, there they grow,
Into the wonders that they soon shall know.
And Sedges, the most handsome he became,
A glance of him portrayed but only fame.
Of shining golden light his fit eyes glow,
And hair that veiled his ears, were white as snow.
And of him was thus asked to stay from sight,
Closed in the tree for soon come his delight.
And Rose grew humble, loving, but yet strong,
Her hair with reds had shimmered with perms long.
Her twinly eyes was hazel pure, that so
Her brother of her trust had come to show.
Nymphaea, th' upright and who water prize,
Who calmly saw the truth in any eyes.
Her hair was blacker as the ace of spades,
Her eyes azure as her fair name pervades.
And brave and serious she was with grins,
Her legs exposed to water turned to fins.
Tillandsia was always found at high,
Her wings made her close friends with the pale sky.
Her hair grew long with woven plaits of gold,

And eyes as green as emeralds behold.
And hopeful she's of any given task,
With grace and elegance without a mask.

28. Hortus' Teachings

THUS, there at every given night, she spoke
To them of stories old that them awoke.
The first was that about creation's fare:
How they at first made all and all declare.
The second was then to enlighten them,
Foretelling them of the great coming gem:

"My children. One day I shall be no more,
And yet in you shall I remain restore,
For soon you shall continue in my ways,
For in this realm that you must fairly raise.
And raise not your concern or fear and doubt,
For I shall teach you of this way devout:
For one must hope at first, for all things come
Of hope before it's true; for hope's ne'er numb.
So look into the eye of hope and see,
That every possible of things could be,
And feel and think and speak and act as one,
And then you'll see a new world thus begun.
But yet of this remain aware of love,
For beauty pure and goodness be above."

29. Rose and Sedges

FOR Rose and Sedges grew-up ever near,
He came to ask of her something e'er dear,
For he was not allowed outside the tree,
And all he ever wanted was to see.
Where she agreed to show him his request,
For she couldn't see her brother so depressed.
One evening she took him out to greet
The world that him awaited long to meet.
And Hortus over saw the wilful act,
For maybe Rose could make his heart attract.
Outside she showed him th' other parts of life,
The fruit, the tree that grew but only five.
And there she told him of this sacred key,
Although of it they must forever flee.

30. Significances

THUS, deities of them were made in time,
As goddesses and god, they shall be prime.
The heirs of Hortus in the second realm,
For all they'll do and all they'll overwhelm.

31. The Order of Creation

AND thus, had come th' appointed time and age,
And from the tree they must thus disengage.
And Hortus called the trinity at first,
And said upon them all these well words versed:

"My dearest children, for the time arrived,
There 'waits the realm by you to be contrived,
You must now go apart, each on their way,
To do as I had done in a good sway,
And don't be sad for you will still remain,
Inside each other's hearts as you shall reign."

And so, they parted with their last fare sound,
Into the water, sky and on the ground.

32. Hortus and Sedges

HENCEFORTH, the last remained in the fair tree,
And Hortus took his hand for the agree.

"O Sedges, so your time has come as well,
To see the outside where you will excel."

Thus Sedges saw it at a second stage,
Where he may take his place and so engage.

And so, where after he his work complete,
May he return to the divine elite.

SCROLL V

The Legend surrounding the

SEVERANCES

THUS

The Scroll Marked Severances

[ARGUMENT]

The following events transpired after the creation of the beings. It is, in fact, the introduction to the second part of the *Hortus*, and explains the attempt by the trinity sisters to prevent the disruption of man after Nymphaea's vision of the future. This includes the harvest of the fruit of life, the movements of the tree of life, the transferal of their powers into the sacred arms, and the transferal of power that were the result of their own transformations as consequence.

33. Peace Among the Populations

THUS, now there was an era of goodwill,
As post creation set out to fulfill.
The aeon of descendants thus commenced,
The age the first of gold thus had dispensed.
So, peace and harmony thus set its course,
There were no fatal things such as remorse.

34. The Oracle of Imminence: The Untold Truth

ONE fairest day, yet fairest not for all,
Nymphaea got a sad eye to appal.
She knew not of it nor about its strife,
And thus set out to the one tree of life.
(She knew that it was Hortus' great effort
To make connections for their true support.)
And with one glance upon the bassinet,
There'd come a ghastly basis into set.
And for her cries allowed her tears to fall,
Into a brutal vision to forestall,
There in the bassinet her tears collect,
That twisted, turned and prophecies reflect.
Bewildered, there she glanced of the feared sight,
For what she saw all lay in ruined might.
The Vesica Pisces in dreaded death,
And fire rose to clear all from the breath.
How vengeful lust for blood all will decay,
And hardship sweat that ruin so display.
Where tears of pain cannot portray the cries,
Of all to come, and starting from mere lies.
Thus, swiftly, she had set her novel course,
To tell her sisters of the great remorse.
And swiftly they made hast for a new plan,
To seek prevention of what yet began.

35. Harvest of the Fruit of Life and The Movements of the Tree

AND so had come the first of waves t' avert,
The tree had powers greatly to convert,
And so, they moved it to the great unknowns,
In hortus, where it stood by the three thrones.
A change that brought mortality to Mars.
Yet 'fore the movement of the tree from spars,
The harvest of the fruit of life betide,
One pearl of black the golden sphere supplied.
Which then were cut and split into a pair,
One ruby rock the algae came to bear,
A stone of emerald was kept at high,
Where they 'll were kept from the ill fate to die.

36. The Sacred Arms

THUS next came from a slow and saddened sight,
The origin dismissed of this delight,
The weapons to protect of lasting hope,
Within the terror and the horror scope.
And by the grace of Hortus who had first
Created them thus to destroy the cursed,
To them again be so disposed as once,
To keep the balance from the treated, dunce.
Nymphaea had one gift to thus bestow,
A mighty fork that Lotus came to know.
And of its good and mighty name record,

The Coral made of gold that's his reward.
Its powers over waters were divine,
As even moons were thus to this decline.
Tillandsia made gifts of gold as well,
Yet more had come from her with whom she dwell:
Bulbosa Maxima had come to own,
A two-edged sword as sharp to cut through stone,
And Cyanea was graced a rod of gold,
The name of Fuchsii it came t' uphold.
To Brachycaulos, Gardneri bestowed,
A spear to keep of mercy well a code.
Usneoides was thus Fuego to keep,
Of arrows and a bow to make them leap.
So Butzii had come to hold a whip,
With a long string and a sharp golden tip.
And Andreana came to bear no arms,
For in her was her gift, for all she charms.
The embryophyte, Rose had come and gave,
A sacred arm, for all from vile be safe.
Carnation it was called, the forged sharp sword,
And of salvation that was its reward.
And yet its owner was unknown, for there
Shall come a time for it to choose the heir.
Thus stuck in soil it waits for a pure heart
To finally unleash its po'erful part.
Thus, this the sacred arms came to be,
From the grand might of the fair trinity.

37. Severances: The Worlds Apart

THUS now, the dusk of piece was close at hand,
A time for sisters' to greet and leave of band.
For all that's come and all they had prevent,
They had to separate as they consent.
Howe'er the worlds could still relate in part,
But for the better must be kept apart.

38. Metamorphoses: The Transformation of the Trinity and the Transferal of Power

THUS now in each own world was they all set,
The trinity and for what they offset:
For deities they were, divine weren't they,
For they had given all there po'ers away.
Their powers thus were locked inside the arms
Yet of it only some they kept their charms.
And for their brother who will seek their end,
They had of one last mission to attend:
Thus, where they stood, they came to stand alone,
Yet in each other's hearts they still were known.
Tillandsia had come to lose her wings;
Nymphaea to a fish her alter brings;
And Rose thus went into the woods of deep,
Where a white stag of her was made to keep.

39. The Elements of Pearl

AND there the Elements were sowed about,
Unfixed from each other on Mars throughout.
For yet they needed there their place to stay:
The second realm demanded their survey.
For though together mixed—the portal doom,
His prison to escape and bring but gloom.
Thus fear, the hopes of miscreated things,
Where in the shadows of the night he brings
The darkness there from where his stalks prevail,
And there he whispers to the weak and frail.
He is as real as you make him to be,
Without it he shall never be so free.

40. The Secret Creation

BEFORE his doom and 'fore his weakened state,
Had Sedges too created an ill fate,
From his one gift to him was once bestowed,
A being of fierce fire that he sowed.
Where now they lurk and waited for revenge,
And his creation waited to avenge,
Yet all in all it still laid incomplete,
For yet it needed more to 'come concrete.

CONCLUDING NOTE.

THERE are many questions surrounding what we believe, and very view (if any) answers…

Thus, this concludes the aeons of creation and gives rise to the ancient legends. And though this concludes the mythological background of the scope of the saga, there are still many things concealed. Secrets that need to be revealed. Yet for now, this remains, and it will give much assistance to comprehend the legends to come.

THE END OF
THE GOLDPRINT OF THE ARCHE

GLOSSARY OF CHARACTERS AND ARTIFACTS, AND SETTINGS.

*Note:
The pronunciation of certain character and artifact names is given. The pronunciation of these words is given merely to understand how they were implemented in the rhythm of the poem and is not intended to replace their actual pronunciation.

A

Algae, the race of A race of mermen and mermaids created by Nymphaea.

Andreana (/ˈæn drə ɑː nə/) One of the members of the High Ionantha created by Tillandsia.

B

Botanica Also known as the Third Realm. Created by Hortus before the shaping of the Cosmos and the three worlds.

Brachycaulos (/ˈbrə kɪ kɔ ləs/) One of the members of the High Ionantha created by Tillandsia.

Bulbosa (/bʌlˈboʊ zɑ/) One of the members of the High Ionantha created by Tillandsia.

Butzii (/ˈbut zɪ aɪ/) One of the members of the High Ionantha created by Tillandsia.

C

Carnation The sword created by Rose in the transferal of power.

Coral A golden fork given to Lotus to help him rule over the seas.

Cyanea (/ˈsaɪ ə nɪ ə/) One of the members of the High Ionantha created by Tillandsia.

E

Elements of Pearl, The The fruit of the opposite tree harvested by Sedges in the cursed crusade, as well as the last fruit harvested to render the Algae and Ionantha immortality.

Embryophyte, the race of The race of men and women created by Rose.

F

Fuchsii (/ˈfyu ʃɪ aɪ/) A golden rod given to Cyanea.

Fuego (/ˈfyu goʊ/) The bow and arrows given to Usneoides.

G

Gardneri A golden spear given to Brachycaulos.

Goldprint of the Arche, the (*also shortened and referred to in the poem as* the Goldprint) The print found in the Realm of Hope and used for creational purposes.

H

Hortus The prime mover and original creator of Botanica and the Second Realm.

I

Infernal Brigade, the The rebellion against the views of Hortus.

Ionantha, the race of (/ˈaɪ oʊ nən θə/) A race of beings with wings created by Tillandsia to live in the sky and clouds.

L

Lotus The first merman created by Nymphaea to rule over the sea.

M

Maxima (/ˈmæk sə mə/) A two-edged sword given to Bulbosa.

N

Nymphaea (/nɪˈfi ə/) One of the members of the Vesica Pisces. The creator of the world under water.

R

Realm of Hope, The The unseen realm. Also, where Sedges is imprisoned.

Rose One of the members of the Vesica Pisces. The creator of the lands of Mars.

S

Sacred arms, The A series of arms given to some beings (created by the trinity sisters) for means of protection and preservation of peace.

Sedges A member of the Vesica Pisces and the leader of the rebellion; creator of the Cosmos excluding Mars.

T

Tetrad siblings, The *See* Vesica Pisces.

The Second Realm The Cosmos, including Mars, created by the Vesica Pisces.

Tillandsia A member of the Vesica Picsces and the creator of the Ionantha.

Tree of Life, The The tree bearing the fruit of life.

Trinity sisters, The The three *sisters* forming part of the Vesica Pisces.

U

Usneoides (/ʌsˈni oʊ aɪ diz/) A member of the High Ionantha, created by Tillandsia.

V

Velvet Gate, The A Velvet curtain behind which the Goldprint of the Arche is put.

Vesica Pisces, The The creators of the second realm. I.e., Rose, Sedges, Nymphaea, Tillandsia

INDEX OF TITLES.

R

S

T

V

INDEX OF FIRST LINES.

O

S

T

W

SIT LAVS DEO PATRI

Milton Keynes UK
Ingram Content Group UK Ltd.
UKHW010625291123
433416UK00005B/341